SCHIRMER'S LIBRARY OF MUSICAL CLASSICS

FREDERIC CHOPIN

Complete Works for the Piano

Edited and Fingered,
and provided with an Introductory Note by

CARL MIKULI

Historical and Analytical Comments by

JAMES HUNEKER

ISBN 978-7935-5261-0

G. SCHIRMER, Inc.

DISTRIBUTED BY

7777 W. BLUEMOUND RD. P.O. BOX 13819 MILWAUKEE, WI 53213

Printed in the U.S.A. by G. Schirmer, Inc.

THE POLONAISES

CHOPIN wrote fifteen Polonaises, the authenticity of one (in G flat major) being doubted by Dr. Niecks. This list includes the Polonaise for piano and violoncello, opus 3—which doesn't come within our study of the solo music—and the Polonaise, opus 22, for piano and orchestration; a consideration of the latter will be found in the volume of this series entitled "Four Concert Pieces." Read by all means the gorgeous description of the Polonaise written by Liszt—aided by Princess Wittgenstein—in his monograph on Chopin. Originating during the last half of the sixteenth century, the Polonaise at first was a measured procession of nobles and their ladies to the sound of music. At the court of Henry of Anjou, in 1574, after his election to the Polish throne, the Polonaise was born and throve in the hardy and warlike atmosphere of the time. It became a dance political, and even had words set to it. It is really a march, a processional dance, grave, moderate, flowing, and seldom stereotyped. Liszt speaks of the capricious life infused into its courtly measures by the Polish aristocracy. It is at once the symbol of war and love, a vivid pageant of martial splendor, a weaving, cadenced, voluptuous dance, the pursuit of half shy, half coquettish women by the fierce warrior. The Polonaise is in three-four time, with the accent on the second beat of the bar. In simple binary form—ternary if a trio is added—this dance has feminine endings to all the principal cadences. The rhythmic cast of the bass is seldom changed. Despite its essentially masculine mould it is given a feminine title; formerly it was called Polonais. A long list of composers with names ending in "ski" have, besides Chopin, contributed to the literature of the form: Kosciusko, Oginski, Moniuszko, Dobrzynski, Kurpinski, Wieniawski, Zarembski, Stojowski, and Paderewski. Liszt wrote two Polonaises of distinction, though like his brilliant Mazurka they smack more of the pompous Magyar than the subtle Pole.

How is one to reconcile the "want of manliness, moral and intellectual," which Hadow asserts is "the one great limitation of Chopin's province," with the power, splendor and courage of the Polonaises? Here are the "cannon buried in flowers" of Robert Schumann's memorable phrase; here overwhelming evidences of virility, versatility and passion. Chopin seems to have blinded his critics and admirers alike as to his true nature. He, too, had his "dæmon" as well as Liszt; and only, as Ehlert puts it, his "theoretical fear" of this spirit's driving him over the precipice of reason made him curb its antics. After all the *couleur de rose* portraits and lollipop miniatures made of him by romantic writers it is difficult to conceive Chopin as irascible, almost brutal; yet he was occasionally both. "Beethoven was scarce more vehement and irritable," writes Ehlert. And we recall the stories of friends and pupils who saw this slender, refined Pole wrestling with his wrath as if obsessed by a devil. Chopin left compositions that bear witness to his masculine side. Puny in person, bad temper ill became him; his education and tastes were opposed to scenes of violence. So this energy, spleen and raging at fortune found escape in some of his music, in it his manifestations became psychical. But—one may object—this is feminine hysteria, the impotent cries of an unmanly, weak nature! The answer is, read the E flat minor, the C minor, A major, F sharp minor and the two A flat major Polonaises. Chopin was weak in physique, but he had the soul of a lion. Allied to the most exquisite poetic sensibility—we are minded here of Balzac's "le beau génie est moins un musicien qu'une âme qui se rend sensible"—there was another nature, fiery, implacable. He loved Poland. He hated her oppressors. There is no doubt that he idealized his country and her wrongs until the pictures grew out of proportion. Politically the Poles and Celts rub shoulders. Niecks points out that if Chopin was "a flattering idealist as a national poet, as a personal poet he was an uncompromising realist." In the Polonaises, therefore, we find two distinct groups: In one, the objective, martial side predominates; in the other is the moody, mournful, morose Chopin. But in all the Polish element pervades; barring the Mazurkas, these dances are the most Polish of his works. An appreciation of Chopin's wide diversity of temperament would have spared the world the false, silly, distorted portraits of him. He had in him the warrior, though he seldom shows the mailed fist, but there are moments when he discards gloves and soft phrases and deals blows that reverberate with a formidable clangor.

Let us begin our survey with the C sharp minor Polonaise, opus 26, which has had the misfortune of being sentimentalized to a sugary death. What can be more *appassionato* than the opening with its "grand, rhythmical swing"? It is usually played in a timid fashion, though a *fortissimo* stares one in the face. The first three lines are heroic, but indignation soon melts into an apathetic humor. After the return and repetition of the theme we are given a genuine love-motive tender enough wherewith to woo a princess. On this the Polonaise closes, a curious ending for such a fiery opening. In no such mood does the E flat minor Polonaise, opus 26, No. 2, begin. It is variously known as the Siberian, the Revolt, and it breathes defiance and rancor. What suppressed and threatening rumblings are on the first sinister page; volcanic mutterings all the more suggestive because of the injunction to open *pianissimo*. One wishes that the shrill high G flat had been written in full chords, as the theme rather suffers from an absence of massiveness. Then follows a subsidiary, but the principal subject relentlessly returns. The episode in B major gives a breathing pause. It has a hint of Meyerbeer. But again with smothered explosions the Polonaise proper reappears and all ends in gloom and the clanking of chains. It is positively awe-evoking, this terrible Polonaise. It was published in 1836.

Not so the celebrated A major Polonaise, opus 40, surnamed "Le Militaire." To Rubinstein this seems a picture of Poland's greatness, as its companion is of Poland's downfall. Although Karasowski and Kleczynski give to the A flat Polonaise (opus 53) the credit of a well-known anecdote, it is really this "Militaire" in A major that deserves it; at least so the Polish portrait painter Kwiatowski informed Niecks. The story runs that after composing the Polonaise Chopin was surprised, terrified in the dreary stretches of the night by the opening of his door and the entrance of a long train of Polish nobles and ladies, all richly robed, who slowly moved by him. Troubled by the ghosts he had raised the hollow-eyed composer fled his apartment in the chateau at Nohant. This incident must have occurred at Majorca, for the opus was composed or else finished there. Ailing, weak and unhappy, as he was, Chopin had grit enough to file and polish this brilliant and striking composition into its present shape. It is the best known and most muscular of his dances, and has something of the festive glitter of Weber. It was published in 1840. The second of the set, the C minor Polonaise, is a noble, yet troubled composition, deeply felt, large in accent. Can anything be more impressive than the opening. Truly Poland's downfall. The A flat trio, with its kaleidoscopic modulations, produces an impression of vague unrest and suppressed sorrow. There are daring and loftiness of spirit throughout the work.

What can I say new of the tremendous Polonaise in F sharp minor? (It was published November, 1841, and is opus 44 in the list.) It is semi-barbaric, it is perhaps pathologic, and of it Liszt has written most eloquent things. For him it is a dream-poem, the "lurid hour that precedes a hurricane," with a "convulsive shudder at the close." The opening is impressive, the nerves harassed by the gradually swelling prelude; there is defiant power in the first theme, and the constant reference to it betrays the composer's exasperated mental condition. This tendency to tormenting introspection, this recoil upon

himself, signifies a grave state of mind. But consider the musical weight of the work, the recklessly bold outpourings of a soul well-nigh distraught. There is no greater touchstone for a poet-pianist than the F sharp minor Polonaise. It is profoundly ironical—else what signifies the apparition of that lovely Mazurka, "a flower between two abysses" (as von Bülow said of the middle movement in the "Moonlight Sonata"). This strange dance is ushered in by two of the most enigmatic pages of Chopin. The A major *intermezzo*, with its booming canons and overtones, is not easily defensible as to form, yet it unmistakably fits in the picture. The Mazurka is charged with interrogations and nuances. The return of the tempest is not long delayed. It bursts, then wanes, and with the *coda* comes sad yearning, and the savage drama tremblingly passes into the night after fluid and wavering affirmations. A roar in F sharp follows the cessation of an agitating nightmare. No "sabre dance," this, but a confession from the depths of a self-tortured temperament.

The A flat Polonaise, opus 53, was published December, 1843, and by Karasowski is said to have been composed in 1840, after Chopin's return from Majorca. This Polonaise is not as feverish, as exalted, as the previous one. It is, as Kleczynski writes, "the type of a war song." There is imaginative splendor in this thrilling work, with its thunders of horse-hoof and fierce challengings. What fire, what smoke and sword-thrusts and clash of mortal conflict! Here is no psychical presentation, but an objective picture of battle, of concrete contours, and united to a cleaving brilliancy in execution that excites the blood to boiling pitch. That Chopin with his frail physique ever played it seems incredible, for none but the heroes of the keyboard can grasp its dense chordal masses, its fiery projectiles of tone. Yet, there is something disturbing, even ghostly, in the *intermezzo* that separates the trio from the return of the first theme; in it are mist and starlight. The work is as a rule taken at too rapid a *tempo*, and on that account is nicknamed the Drum Polonaise, thus losing in force and stateliness because of the vanity of *virtuosi*. Again, the octaves in E are usually spun out as if speed were the sole motive of this episode. Do not sacrifice the Polonaise to the octaves! As powerful a battle tableau as it is, still it may be presented so as not to shock our sense of the euphonious, or betray the limitations of the instrument. When arranged for orchestra this composition becomes vapid and unheroic. Its measures demand the sharp percussions of the piano.

The Polonaise-Fantaisie in A flat, opus 61, was given to the world in September, 1846. One of the three great Polonaises, it is only beginning to be understood, having been derided as febrile, amorphous, of little moment; even Liszt declares that "such pictures possess but little real value to art.

Deplorable visions which the artist should admit with extreme circumspection within the graceful circle of his charmed realm." This was written in the old-fashioned days when art was "aristocratic" and attempted to exclude the "baser" and more drastic emotions. For a generation accustomed to the realism of Richard Strauss the Fantaisie-Polonaise seems vaporously fantastic. It reminds me of one of those enchanted flasks of the Eastern magi from which, on opening, a smoke exhales that gradually forms itself into terrible and fearsome shapes. This Polonaise at no time exhibits the solidity of its two predecessors; its plasticity defies the imprint of the conventional dance, though we always feel its rhythmic life; the units of style and structure are in it. It was music of the future when composed. But the realism is a trifle cloudy. Here is the duality of Chopin the suffering man, and Chopin the prophet of Poland. There are shifting lights and shadows, restless tonalities, but the end is triumphant, recalling in key and climax the A flat Ballade.

Opus 71, three posthumous Polonaises, preserved by Julius Fontana, are in D minor, published in 1827, B flat, May, 1828, and F minor, 1829. They are interesting to Chopinists. The influence of Weber, a past master in this form, is felt. Of the three, the last in F minor is the strongest, though if Chopin's age is taken into consideration, the first, in D minor, is quite an accomplished feat for a lad of eighteen. I agree with Niecks that the posthumous Polonaise in G sharp minor was composed later than 1822—the date given in the Breitkopf and Härtel edition. It is in artistic conception and "light-winged figuration" far more mature than the Chopin of opus 71. Really a graceful and effective little composition of the florid order, but like most of his early music without poetic depth. A facsimile reproduction of a hitherto unpublished Polonaise in A flat was published in the Warsaw "Echo Musicale" to commemorate the fiftieth anniversary of Chopin's death. Written at the age of eleven, this tiny dance is a tentative groping after the form he later conquered so magnificently.

Two Polonaises remain. One, in B flat minor, was composed in 1826, on the occasion of the composer's departure for Reinerz. A footnote to the edition of this rather elegiac piece records this title: "Adieu à Guillaume Kolberg," and the trio in D flat is accredited to an air from "La Gazza Ladra," with a sentimental "au revoir" inscribed. Kleczynski revised this dance. The little cadenza in chromatic double-notes is surely Chopin. But the Polonaise in G flat, published by Schott, is doubtful. It has a shallow ring, a brilliant superficiality, that warrants Niecks in stamping it as a possible compilation. There are scanty traces of the master—most of all in the E flat minor trio; there are also some clumsy progressions and a flavor of commonplace certainly not of Chopin. Beethoven, Schubert, Weber, Bach—in his B minor Suite for strings and flute—all indulged in this dance-form. As a student Wagner wrote a Polonaise for four hands, in the key of D, and at the close of the "Papilions" of Schumann there is a charming specimen. Rubinstein composed a brilliant and dramatic example in E flat, for his "Le Bal," and Liszt's contributions have been already noted. Before Chopin the Weber Polonaise was the most interesting, but the master of all is the Sarmatian composer.

James Huneker

Thematic Index.

Deux Polonaises.

à Mr J. DESSAUER.

F. CHOPIN. Op. 26, No 1.

Allegro appassionato.

11471 r

Fine.

Polonaise da Capo al Fine.

Polonaise.

F. CHOPIN. Op. 26, № 2.

*) While Mme. Rubio was studying this 2nd Polonaise with Chopin, he wrote with his own hand in her copy (in divergence from the books of the other pupils) at this passage and its repetition, a ♮ instead of a ♭ before D.

Deux Polonaises.

a M.ᵣ J. FONTANA.

F. CHOPIN. Op. 40, № 1.

Allegro con brio.

Polonaise.

Allegro maestoso.

F. CHOPIN. Op. 40, № 2.

Polonaise.

à Mme la Princesse CH. de BEAUVAU.

F. CHOPIN. Op. 44.

Doppio movimento: (Tempo di Mazurka.)

Tempo I. *(di Polacca.)*

Polonaise.

a Mr. A. LEO.

F. CHOPIN, Op. 53.

11476

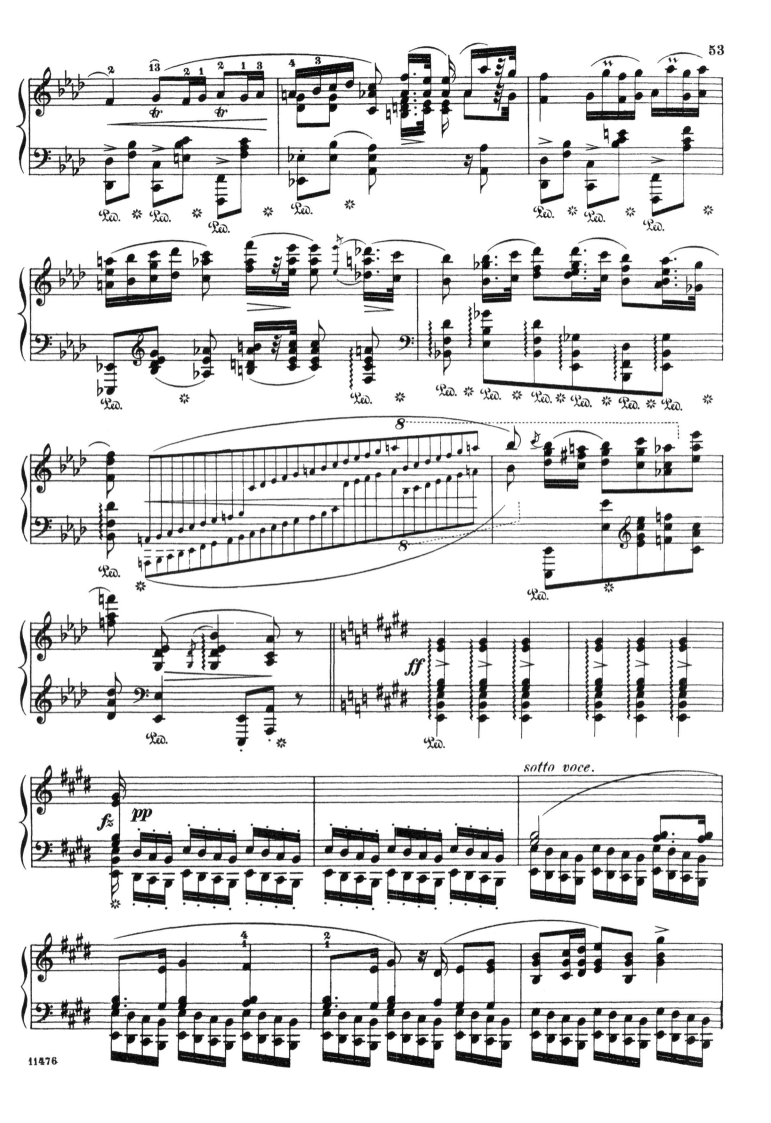

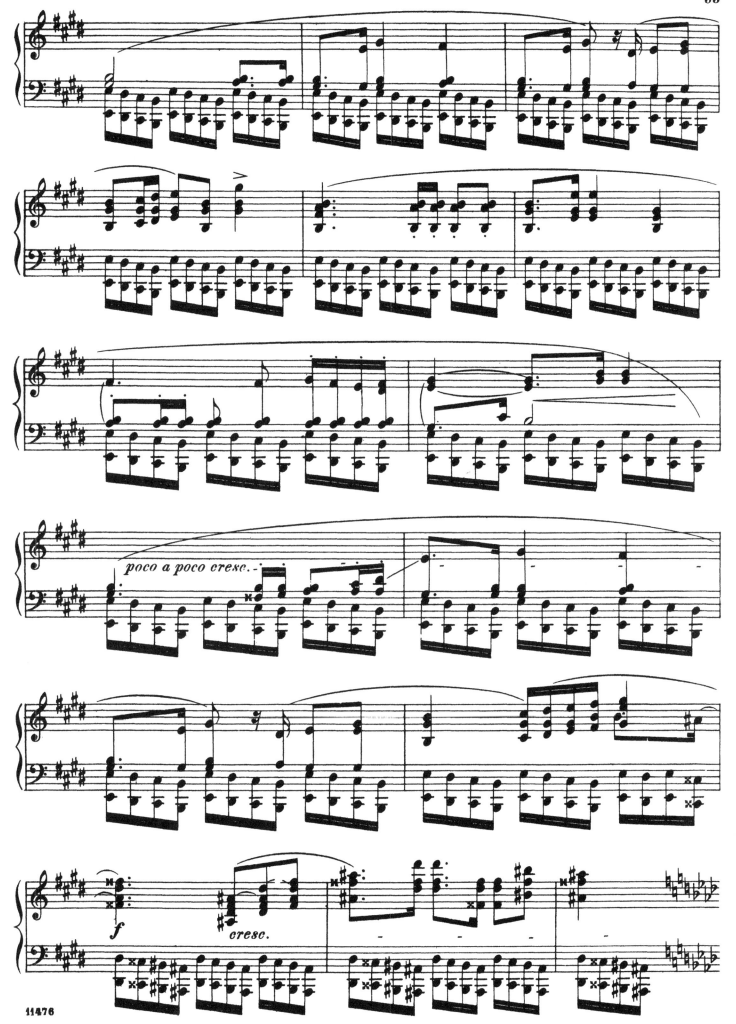

Polonaise-Fantaisie.

à Mme A. VAYRET.

F. CHOPIN. Op. 61.

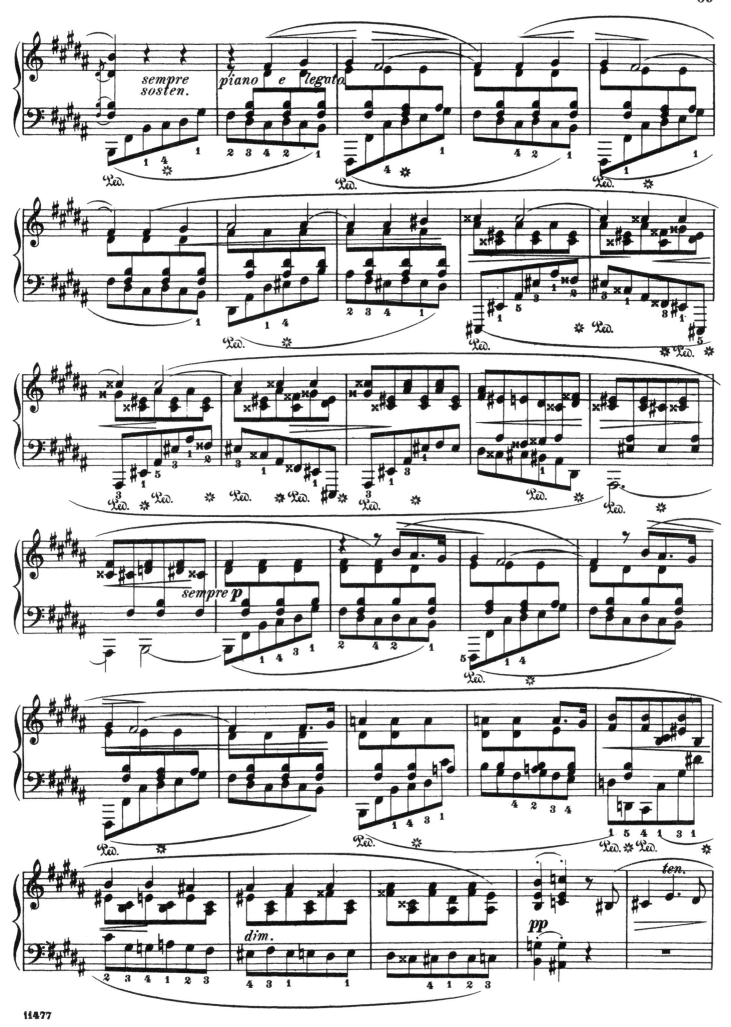

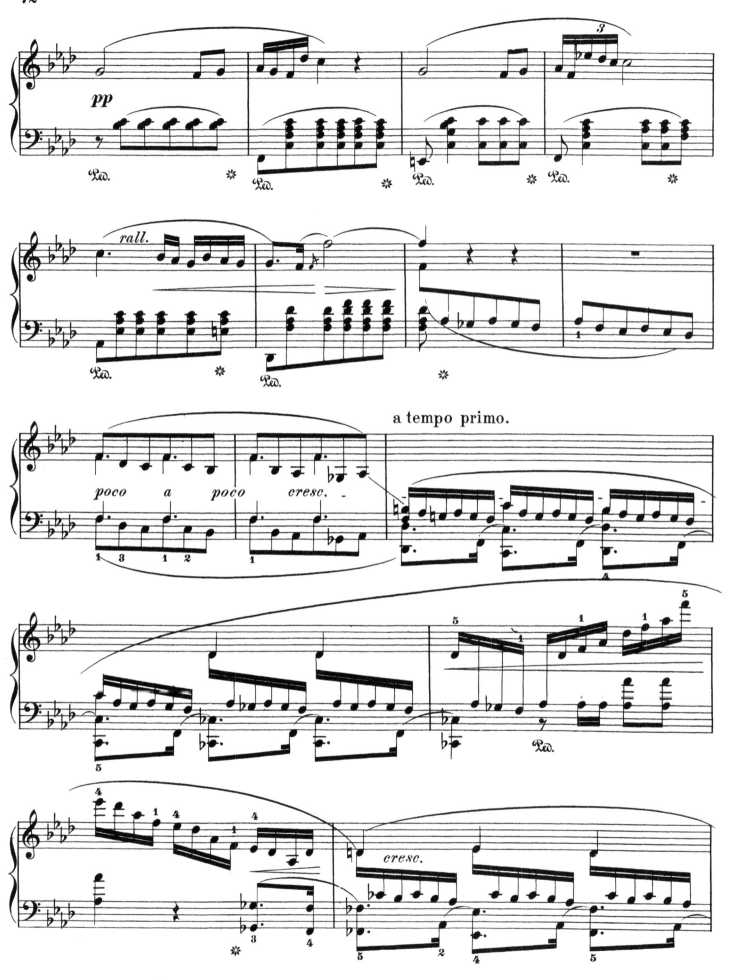

Polonaise.

(Posthumous.)

F. CHOPIN. Op.71. № 1.
(1827)

11478

10

Polonaise.
(Posthumous.)

Allegro, ma non troppo. (♩ = 92.)

F. CHOPIN. Op. 71, № 2.
(1828.)

Polonaise.

(Posthumous.)

F. CHOPIN. Op. 71, No 3.
(1829.)

11480

11486

Polonaise.

(Posthumous.)

Moderato.

F. CHOPIN.

11.

4